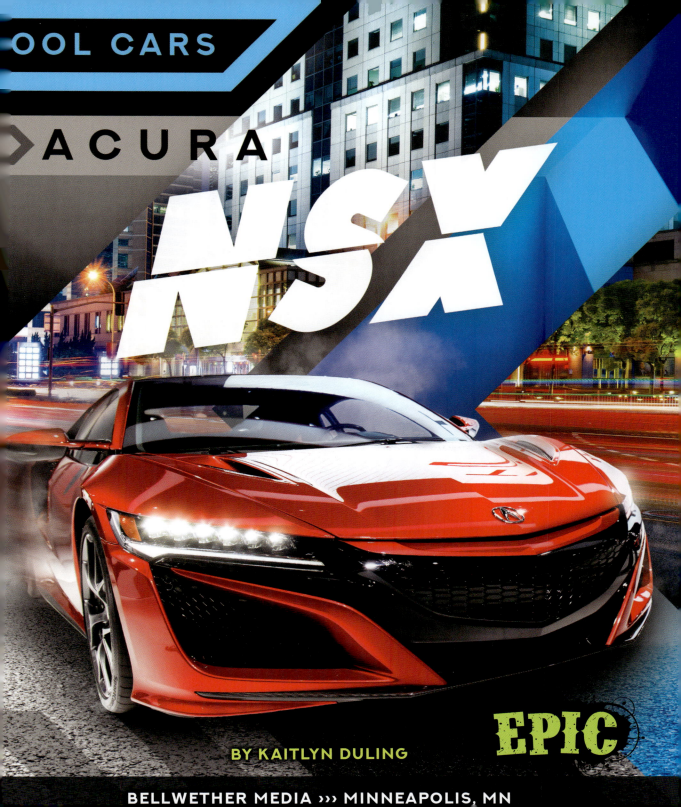

COOL CARS

ACURA NSX

BY KAITLYN DULING

EPIC

BELLWETHER MEDIA ››› MINNEAPOLIS, MN

EPIC BOOKS are no ordinary books. They burst with intense action, high-speed heroics, and shadows of the unknown. Are you ready for an Epic adventure?

This edition first published in 2023 by Bellwether Media, Inc.

No part of this publication may be reproduced in whole or in part without written permission of the publisher. For information regarding permission, write to Bellwether Media, Inc., Attention: Permissions Department, 6012 Blue Circle Drive, Minnetonka, MN 55343.

Library of Congress Cataloging-in-Publication Data

LC record for Acura NSX available at: https://lccn.lcc.gov/2022044260

Text copyright © 2023 by Bellwether Media, Inc. EPIC and associated logos are trademarks and/or registered trademarks of Bellwether Media, Inc.

Editor: Rachael Barnes   Designer: Jeffrey Kollock

Printed in the United States of America, North Mankcto, MN

TABLE OF CONTENTS

SILENTLY SPEEDING BY	4
ALL ABOUT THE NSX	6
PARTS OF THE NSX	12
THE NSX'S FUTURE	20
GLOSSARY	22
TO LEARN MORE	23
INDEX	24

SILENTLY SPEEDING BY

The Acura NSX zooms down the road. It passes car after car. It stands out on the city streets.

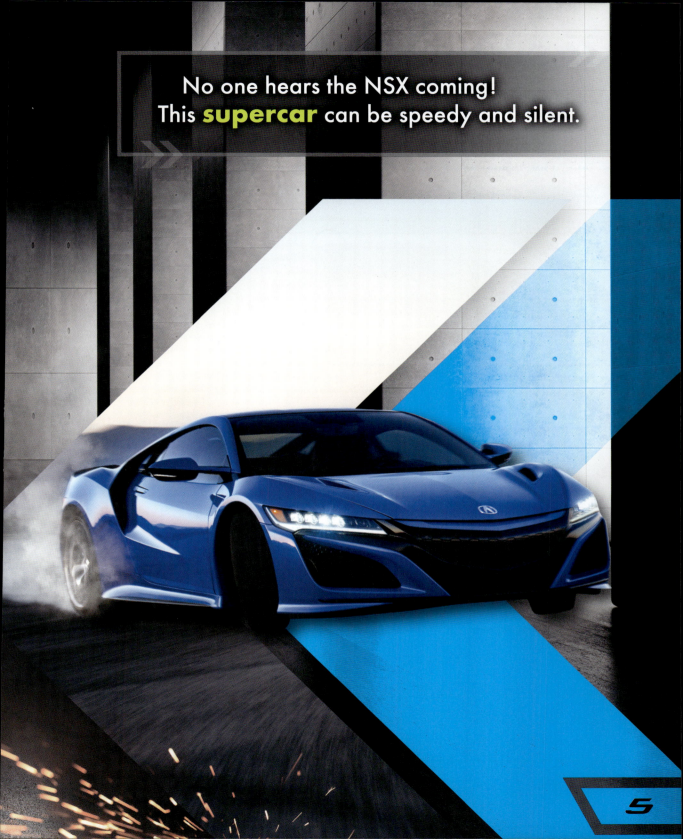

ALL ABOUT THE NSX »

**HONDA MOTOR COMPANY
TOKYO, JAPAN**

Acura is part of the Honda Motor Company. They launched Acura in 1986. Acura created the first Japanese-made **luxury** cars sold in the United States.

Acura became known for making safe supercars.

The NSX was first presented in 1989. For years, it was built by hand in Marysville, Ohio.

FIRST NSX AT THE 1989 CHICAGO AUTO SHOW

The NSX is a **coupe**. It can be driven on a racetrack or on a road trip.

⚲ WHERE IS IT MADE?

UNITED STATES

MARYSVILLE, OHIO

The NSX Type S released in 2022. It is the most powerful Acura yet!

The NSX comes with all-wheel drive. This helps it turn. A nine-speed **automatic transmission** helps it drive smoothly.

NAME GAME

NSX stands for "New Sportscar eXperience."

NSX TYPE S

ACURA NSX BASICS

YEAR FIRST MADE — 1990

COST — starts at $171,495

HOW MANY MADE — 350 of the 2022 Type S

FEATURES

- dome-shaped cockpit
- front grille
- LED headlights

PARTS OF THE NSX

The NSX is a **hybrid**. It has a **V6 engine** paired with three **electric motors**. It can reach 60 miles (97 kilometers) per hour in 2.9 seconds!

ENGINE SPECS

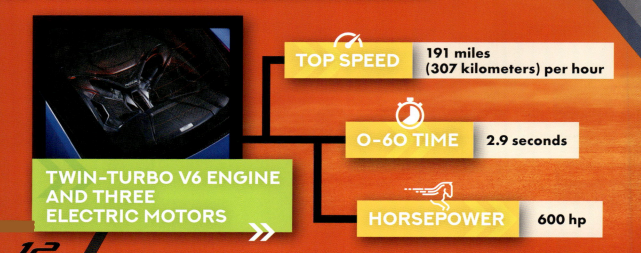

TWIN-TURBO V6 ENGINE AND THREE ELECTRIC MOTORS

TOP SPEED — 191 miles (307 kilometers) per hour

0-60 TIME — 2.9 seconds

HORSEPOWER — 600 hp

The car's body is made of lightweight **carbon fiber**. Its **LED** headlights light up the night.

LED HEADLIGHT

SIZE CHART

WIDTH 76.3 inches (193.8 centimeters)

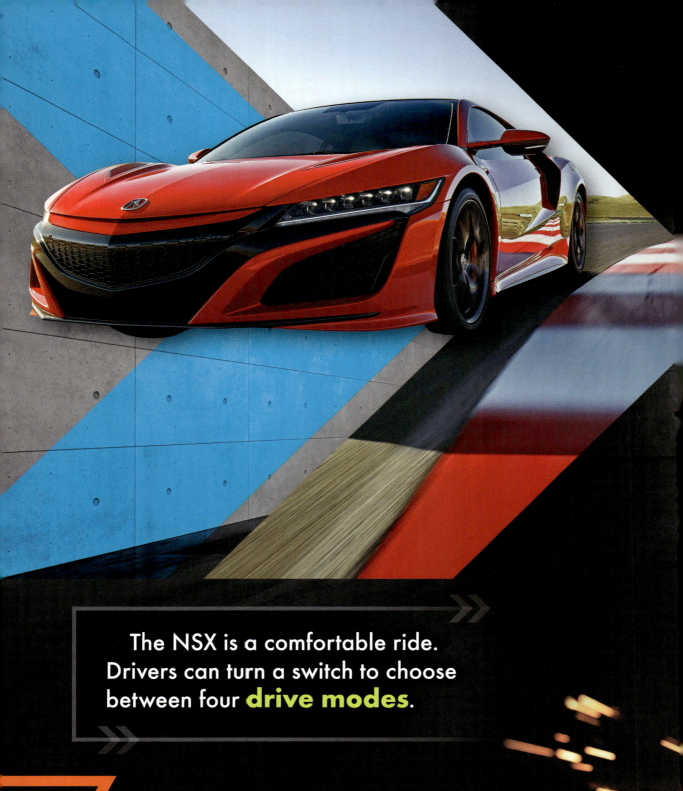

The NSX is a comfortable ride. Drivers can turn a switch to choose between four **drive modes**.

Quiet mode uses only the electric motors. Other modes give the driver more control. They can make sharper turns!

IN THE PILOT'S SEAT

Drivers sit in the NSX's dome-shaped cockpit. This area was made to look and feel like an F-16 fighter jet!

DOME-SHAPED COCKPIT

Drivers can **customize** the NSX. They can choose body and seat colors.

18

They can even pay for lighter parts.
These can help the NSX speed up even faster.

THE NSX'S FUTURE »

Acura stopped making the NSX in 2022. But the company plans to make more hybrid and electric cars.

Future Acura tech will recognize the faces of drivers and passengers. Acuras will be smart cars!

GLOSSARY

automatic transmission—a car part that shifts gears for the driver

carbon fiber—a strong, lightweight material used to strengthen things

coupe—a car with a hard roof and two doors

customize—to make to personal order

drive modes—settings in cars that change how the car drives for different tasks

electric motors—parts in cars that produce power using batteries

grille—a set of bars that cover an opening on the front of a car; the grille allows air to enter and exit.

hybrid—using both a gasoline engine and an electric motor for power

LED—a type of light that saves energy and takes a very long time to burn out

luxury—having a high level of comfort

supercar—an expensive and high performing sports car

V6 engine—an engine with 6 cylinders arranged in the shape of a "V"

TO LEARN MORE

AT THE LIBRARY
Adamson, Thomas K. *Sports Cars*. Minneapolis, Minn.: Bellwether Media, 2019.

Peterson, Megan Cooley. *Acura NSX*. Mankato, Minn.: Black Rabbit Books, 2021.

Swanson, Jennifer. *How Do Hybrid Cars Work?* Mankato, Minn.: The Child's World, 2022.

ON THE WEB

FACTSURFER

Factsurfer.com gives you a safe, fun way to find more information.

1. Go to www.factsurfer.com.

2. Enter "Acura NSX" into the search box and click 🔍.

3. Select your book cover to see a list of related content.

INDEX

Acura, 6, 7, 10, 20
all-wheel drive, 10
automatic transmission, 10
basics, 11
body, 14, 18
carbon fiber, 14
cockpit, 17
colors, 18
coupe, 9
drive modes, 16, 17
electric motors, 12, 17
engine, 12, 15
engine specs, 12
future, 20
grille, 15
headlights, 14
history, 6, 8, 10, 20
Honda Motor Company, 6
hybrid, 12, 20

Marysville, Ohio, 8, 9
name, 10
NSX Type S, 10
size chart, 14–15
speed, 4, 5, 12, 19
supercar, 5, 7

The images in this book are reproduced through the courtesy of: Miro Vrlik Photography/ Alamy, front cover; Acura, pp. 3, 4, 5, 7, 8, 9, 10, 11, 12, 13, 14, 15, 16, 17, 18, 19, 20, 21; Aflo Co. Ltd./ Alamy, p. 6.